SPARKLING STARS
AND BRAVE HEARTS

BEDTIME STORIES FOR BABIES,
TODDLERS AND KIDS.

Foreword

Dear little and big readers,

In your hands, you hold a book full of magic, baptized "Sparkling Stars and Brave Hearts." Every story hidden within these pages is a window into a world where the twinkle of stars and the courage of hearts go hand in hand. As children, we often gaze up at the night sky and wonder what lies beyond those sparkling stars. Each star you will find here tells a story - of adventures, of dreams, of small beings with great courage. This book is meant to serve not only as a companion for bedtime but also as inspiration for those young hearts who are just learning to be brave, to overcome their fears, and to chase their dreams. It is a reminder that, no matter how big or small we are, within each of us beats a courageous heart ready to shine. I invite you to explore this book page by page, star by star. Find solace in the gentle narratives and let the heroines and heroes you will meet inspire you. May the stories in "Sparkling Stars and Brave Hearts" illuminate your nights and fill your dreams with hope and courage.

Bedtime Stories

The Penguin and the Unknown	4
The Journey of the Brave Rabbit	6
The Curious Owl	8
Raccoon Max	10
The Tale of the Snail and Time	12
Leo, the Tree Spider	14
The Dancing Turtle	16
The Melody-less Wolf	18
Ben and the Stardust	20
The Gentle Butterfly	22
Florian's Starry Pond	24
Rosa Dances in the Starlight	26
The Elephant and the Stardust	28
The Dreaming Fox	30
Anton and the Moon Song	32
The Little Mouse	34
Vivi and the Moon	36
The Brave Squirrel	38

The Penguin and the Unknown

In the icy shimmering expanses of Antarctica lived a special penguin named Pauline. Pauline was known for her shiny black and white plumage that stood out amidst the snow and ice. She was happy and content in her small colony, but she had always dreamed of the unexplored areas beyond her home.

One day, Pauline decided that she was ready to explore the unknown territories of Antarctica. The other penguins warned her about the dangers and secrets of the icy wilderness, but Pauline was not fearful. She was curious and adventurous, wanting to see the beauty that lay beyond her familiar surroundings.

With determined steps, Pauline waddled deeper into the land of ice. The farther she went, the colder and stormier it became. Amidst a snowstorm, she began to discover new and astonishing things. She saw strange and wonderful creatures she had never seen before, like glittering ice worms and luminous swarms of krill.

During her journey, Pauline encountered a huge, friendly seal who showed her the wonders of the icy continent. Together, they discovered deep glacier crevasses, impressive ice sculptures, and breathtaking snowscapes.

Pauline was thrilled by all the new experiences and insights. After some time, she returned to her colony.

She was full of stories and knowledge that she shared with the other penguins. Everyone listened eagerly as Pauline recounted her adventures in the icy wilderness. She explained that it was beautiful and teeming with life, despite being cold and challenging.

The story of Pauline the penguin teaches us that there is a wonderful world to discover if we have the courage to explore the unknown. It shows us the joy of discovery and reminds us that a spirit of adventure is a way to gain new experiences and expand our understanding of the world.

The Journey of the Brave Rabbit

In the heart of a lush, green forest lived a fluffy rabbit named Finn. Finn had a best friend, a little hedgehog named Ignatz, who unfortunately was very sick.

Ignatz hadn't been the cheerful, energetic hedgehog he once was for a long time. He had grown weak and could hardly play with Finn anymore. The wise old fox said that only a special medicine, which grew at the other end of the forest, could heal Ignatz. But the path there was dangerous and full of unknown perils.

Finn was initially fearful. He was a small rabbit, and the forest was a vast, intimidating place. But then he saw his friend, who looked so frail and suffering, and he knew he had to try. For Ignatz. For the friendship they shared.

With a brave heart and a firm determination, Finn set out on the journey. He hopped through dense bushes, leaped over swiftly flowing streams, and climbed over high hills. He encountered huge grumbling bears and slithering lurking snakes. Yet, Finn didn't let himself be intimidated. He thought of Ignatz and found the courage to keep going.

After many days and nights filled with challenges, Finn finally reached the other end of the forest. There, beneath an old, gnarled tree, he found the special medicine - a shiny golden flower that glowed in the moonlight. With the beautiful flower safely tucked in his small backpack, Finn began the journey back.

He felt tired and exhausted, but the image of Ignatz waiting for him gave him strength.

When Finn finally arrived back home, the whole forest was in a commotion. Everyone had been worried about the rabbit, and they were overjoyed to see him back in good health. They cheered even louder when they saw that he had found the golden flower. The old fox prepared a medicine from the flower and gave it to Ignatz. It didn't take long for Ignatz to start feeling better. His energy returned, and soon he could laugh and play again.

The animals in the forest celebrated Finn as a hero. But in his heart, he didn't feel like a hero - he was just a friend. A friend who would do anything to help the one he loved. That was the greatest test of courage of all.

The Curious Owl

Once upon a time, there was a little owl named Luna who lived in an old, gnarled tree at the heart of the forest. Luna wasn't like the other owls. She was exceptionally curious and always asked questions.

Why is the sky blue? Why does the moon shine at night and not during the day? Why can birds fly while mice can't? Luna wanted to know everything. She perched on her branch, observing the world around her, always in search of answers.

The other animals in the forest marveled at Luna's endless questions. "Why do you ask so much?" they wondered. "Isn't it easier to accept things as they are?" But Luna just shook her head. "I want to understand everything," she said.

And so, Luna set out to find answers. She asked the bees why they collected nectar, and they told her about the importance of pollination. She asked the river why it flowed, and it told her about gravity. She asked the oak tree why it shed its leaves, and the tree told her about the changing seasons.

With every question Luna asked, she became a little wiser. She learned so much about the world around her, and the owl loved sharing this knowledge with the other animals. Soon, the other creatures of the forest came to her when they had questions. They knew that Luna usually had an answer.

In the world of animals, Luna became known as the wise owl. The other animals realized that her curiosity had led her to knowledge and wisdom. They saw that it wasn't bad to ask questions, but rather a way to learn more about the world and better understand how things worked.

And so, Luna taught all the animals in the forest the importance of asking questions and curiosity. It's often those who ask that learn the most.

Raccoon Max

In a dense, green forest lived a little raccoon named Max. Max had the habit of washing his shiny paws in a nearby stream before falling asleep. But today, the stream reflected the moonlight in a particularly magical way, as if inviting him to a mysterious adventure.

As Max dipped his paws into the water, he suddenly felt very tired. His eyes grew heavy, and before he knew it, he had sunk into a deep dream.

He dreamt that the stream took him on a wondrous journey. Max floated over the water and became smaller and smaller until he was light enough to land on a lily pad that looked like a tiny boat. A cheerful frog hopped over to him, introduced himself as Moritz, and said, "Come, Max, I'll show you the secret Moon Pond!"

The two friends sailed beneath the sky adorned with sparkling stars. They encountered dancing dragonflies that glowed in the darkness and gentle fish that swam beneath them like fluffy clouds.

After a while, they reached the Moon Pond. The water was so clear and silvery that it perfectly reflected the big, round moon. "This is a very special place," Moritz said. "Here, you can make a wish." Max paused for a moment and wished for him and his friends to always be happy and safe.

As he voiced his wish, a gentle breeze swept over the pond, and a soft voice whispered, "Your wish will come true, little raccoon."

With that warm, comforting feeling, Max woke up at the edge of the stream. He knew it had been just a dream, but the sense of solace and security lingered.

The raccoon curled up comfortably, pulled his fluffy tail close, and fell into a deep sleep, dreaming of all the adventures the next day would bring. "And so, my little star, we all find comfort and wonderful dreams in the night. Sleep well."

The Tale of the Snail and Time

IIn a beautiful garden where many animals lived, a little snail named Paul often felt out of sync. All the other animals seemed to always be in a hurry and busy. The birds fluttered through the sky, the squirrels leaped from branch to branch, and the rabbits hopped joyfully around.

Paul, on the other hand, was slow. He moved at his own pace, crawling and gliding, never in a rush. Sometimes, this made the other animals impatient. "Why are you so slow, Paul?" they would ask. "Why don't you hurry like we do?" The snail would simply smile and respond, "Because I love doing things at my own pace."

One day, Paul noticed that Hans, the young rabbit, looked very sad. "What's wrong, Hans?" he asked. The rabbit replied, "I always feel so stressed trying to keep up with everyone else. I don't have time to smell the flowers or enjoy the beauty of the garden."

Paul smiled and said, "You know, Hans, you don't always have to keep up with the others. It's okay to do things at your own pace. You can take time to smell the flowers and enjoy the beauty of the garden. Time is a gift, and it's okay to use it at your own pace."

Hans listened to Paul and took his words to heart. He started taking time to enjoy the garden, smell the flowers, and live life at his own pace.

Thus, the story of the little snail teaches us that it's okay to do things at our own pace and that we don't always have to keep up with others. Life is not a race track but a journey to be savored.

Leo, the Tree Spider

High up in an old oak tree, far away from the bustling world below, Leo, the little spider, built his glistening web. Amidst the green leaves and gnarled branches, he found a perfect spot where the morning light made the delicate threads sparkle.

Unlike many spiders that spent their time in the shadows, Leo loved being in the sun and observing the fluffy clouds in the sky. He relished the chirping of birds and the rustling of leaves.

One day, as a gentle breeze rustled through the leaves, a butterfly named Lila fluttered into Leo's web. "Oh no!" whispered Lila when she realized she was trapped. Leo hurried over and said in a gentle voice, "Don't worry, Lila. I'll help you." With great care, Leo freed the butterfly from the web.

"Thank you, Leo," said Lila with relief. "You truly are a special spider."

From that day on, Lila visited Leo often. She told all the animals in the forest about the friendly tree spider. Soon, many animals came to visit Leo: beetles, crickets, and even a curious squirrel.

When the sun set and the moon and stars twinkled in the sky, Leo nestled into the center of his web, listening to the nocturnal sounds of the forest.

So, dear children, the story of Leo, the tree spider, shows us the value of kindness and that true friendship can be found everywhere. Sleep well and dream sweetly.

The Dancing Turtle

16

In a tranquil pond deep within the forest lived a small turtle named Theo. Theo was different from the other turtles. While they enjoyed spending their time with leisurely swims and sunbathing on a warm rock, Theo had a different passion. He loved to dance.

Every day, when the sun was at its highest and the other animals took their midday rest, Theo would climb onto a flat rock and start to dance. He spun, he twirled, he stretched his tiny legs as far as he could. Theo wasn't the fastest or the most graceful, but that didn't bother him. When he danced, he felt free and happy.

Some of the other animals made fun of him. "Look at the silly turtle," they would laugh. "Turtles shouldn't dance. They're too slow and stiff." But Theo didn't pay them any mind. He loved to dance, and that was all that mattered.

One day, while Theo was dancing, he noticed a movement out of the corner of his eye. He turned around and saw a group of young ducklings watching him with curiosity. "Can you teach us to dance?" one of the ducklings asked.

Theo was surprised, but he beamed with joy. "Of course," he replied, and he began to show the ducklings how to twirl and spin. They laughed and squeaked with delight, their little wings flapping back and forth as they danced.

Gradually, more animals joined in. Squirrels, frogs, deer, and even the old grumpy bear. They all wanted to learn how to dance. And so, Theo taught them to move to the music of the forest—the buzzing of bees, the rustling of the wind, and the splashing of water.

The animals who had once laughed at Theo now saw how much joy his dancing brought to others as well. They realized that it didn't matter how fast or graceful one was. What mattered was the joy, the passion, and the happiness found in doing what one loved.

And so, Theo danced. He danced for himself, he danced for his friends, and he danced for anyone who wanted to discover the joy of dancing. And even though he was a slow, stiff turtle, in the hearts of all the forest creatures, he became the best dancer of them all.

The Melody-less Wolf

IIn the heart of the dense forest lived a young wolf named Loki. In many ways, Loki was like the other wolves - he had a shiny gray coat, sharp claws, and ears that were always attentive. But there was one thing that set Loki apart from the other wolves: he couldn't howl.

The other wolves in his pack could make loud, powerful howling sounds that echoed through the entire forest. No matter how hard Loki tried, he could only produce a soft whimper. The other wolves often made fun of Loki and called him "the silent wolf." He often felt sad and left out.

One day, as Loki tried to howl again and only managed a quiet whimper, he noticed something strange. The birds in the trees stopped singing, and the deer raised their heads curiously. They all listened to Loki. He realized that his soft whimper had a gentle, melodic quality that soothed and captivated the forest animals.

Loki began to experiment with his voice and discovered that he could produce a variety of sounds - some soft and gentle, others deep and warm. But all of them were unique and melodic. The forest animals started to gather around Loki to listen to him. They loved his gentle tones that calmed and fascinated them.

The other wolves noticed what was happening. They saw how Loki, the "silent wolf," impressed the forest animals in a way they never could. They realized that Loki, even though he couldn't howl, had a unique gift that they did not possess.

Loki, who once tried to be like the other wolves, realized that his uniqueness was something to be celebrated, not hidden. He was not just the "silent wolf Loki" - he was the "Wolf of Melodies," and he was proud of it.

Ben and the Stardust

In a blooming garden, surrounded by colorful flowers and buzzing insects, lived Ben, the little bee. Ben wasn't like the other bees. Instead of spending the whole day collecting nectar, he often dreamt of flying in the sky and playing with the stars.

Every night, Ben climbed to the tallest blossom in the garden and watched the twinkling night sky. He imagined what it would be like to fly high up there and touch the stardust.

One night, the bee noticed something falling from the sky. It shimmered and sparkled, landing right at its feet. It was a tiny pile of stardust!

Gently, Ben touched the stardust with its antennae. Suddenly, it felt its wings growing stronger. Without realizing it, it began to fly, higher and higher, until it was among the stars.

The stars danced around him and played with Ben. He felt free and joyful. After a while, though, Ben felt the magic of the stardust fading, and he slowly descended back to the garden.

As the sun rose, the bee was safely back on its favorite flower. Ben knew it was a special adventure he would never forget.

From that day on, Ben told all the insects in the garden about his magical journey to the stars. Every night, before falling asleep, he looked up at the sky, grateful for the wonderful gift of stardust.

Sleep well, little listeners. May your dream be filled with twinkling stars and magical adventures. Good night.

The Gentle Butterfly

In a vibrant garden nestled at the foot of a colossal mountain, lived an exceptionally delicate butterfly named Flora. Flora was more delicate than any other butterfly in the swarm, but what she lacked in size, she compensated with her large heart and unwavering determination.

One day, as the butterflies prepared to gather nectar for the impending winter, Flora made a bold proposition. "I will fly over the mountain and search for the sweetest flowers," she declared. The other butterflies laughed. "You're too delicate, Flora," they said. "You'll never make it to the top."

Flora didn't let herself get discouraged. She knew she was dainty, but she believed in herself and her abilities. Thus, she set out to cross the mountain. The journey was tough. The wind was strong, and the air was cold. But Flora didn't give up. She kept flying and flying, and with each beat of her wings, she grew stronger and more self-assured. She realized that the size of her heart, not the span of her wings, was what truly mattered.

After many days and nights, Flora finally reached the summit of the mountain. She was exhausted but content. From the mountaintop, she could see the entire garden and the vast landscape around it. She felt more liberated and courageous than ever before.

Flora returned to her garden with a smile on her face and a load of sweet nectar. The other butterflies were amazed. "How did you manage that, Flora?" they asked. Flora just smiled and said, "It's not about how delicate you are. It's about how big your heart is."

The story of Flora, the delicate butterfly, teaches us that perseverance and self-confidence can help us overcome the greatest challenges. And that it's not about how big or small we are, but about the size of our heart and how strongly we believe in ourselves.

Florian's Starry Pond

In the heart of a mysterious forest, there was a sparkling pond. There lived Florian, a little green frog with large, twinkling eyes. Florian loved to sit by the pond's edge at night and watch the stars in the sky. He found them so beautiful that he often wished he could see them up close.

One evening, as the frog admired the stars as usual, a small star suddenly fell right into his pond! The star sparkled and glistened in the water, illuminating it.

Florian hopped around joyfully and said, "Hello, little star! Why have you come to me?"

The star replied with a soft, gentle voice, "I wanted to pay you a visit, dear frog. I've seen how you look up at us every night and wanted to bring you some starlight directly into your pond."

Florian was overjoyed and thanked the star. The two quickly became friends and spent the entire night telling stories and singing songs.

As morning broke, the star said to Florian, "It's time for me to return to the sky. But every time you look up at the night sky, you will see me and know that you have a friend up there."

With these words, the star ascended again and found its place among the other stars.

Florian felt grateful and happy to have found such a special friend. Every night, he gazed at the sky, waved to his starry friend, and fell asleep with a smile on his face.

Good night, dear children. Always remember that friends can be found everywhere, even in the sky.

Rosa Dances in the Starlight

In a quiet forest where the pines tickled the sky, lived a young deer named Rosa. Rosa had shining eyes and velvety fur that shimmered in the sunlight.

Although the forest was full of adventures and friends during the day, the deer particularly loved the quiet beauty of the night. When the moon was high and bright in the sky, silver rays streamed onto the forest meadow, and Rosa felt magically drawn.

One evening, when the moon was especially large and radiant, Rosa stepped onto the clearing. The moonbeams transformed the meadow into a sparkling sea of diamonds. She felt a gentle music in the air, the soft whisper of the wind, and the gentle murmur of the nearby stream.

The deer began to dance. First slowly and hesitantly, then more boldly and freely. Rosa spun, leaped, and danced gracefully across the meadow, her heart full of joy.

An owl perched on a branch and watched her. Impressed by her grace, it hooted a soft melody. A few fireflies, drawn by the music, floated over and danced around Rosa, their tiny lights flickering in rhythm.

It was a enchanting sight. The whole nature seemed to dance with Rosa. The stars shone brighter, the stream glittered with starlight, and the trees swayed gently back and forth.

After the last note faded and the final spin was completed, Rosa lay down on the soft grass, tired but content. She closed her eyes and listened to the gentle song of the cicadas.

Dear children, the story of Rosa reminds us to see the beauty around us and to enjoy the moment. Sometimes, the simplest things are the most magical. Good night, and dream beautifully of your own magical dances.

The Elephant and the Stardust

28

In a distant land where the sun shines hot all day long and the nights are cold and clear, lived Enzo, a little elephant. He was no ordinary elephant. Instead of being gray like most elephants, Enzo had a unique deep blue skin. When night fell, tiny silver dots sparkled on his body – it looked as if he carried the night sky on his back.

Enzo loved to take walks at night. The cool sand under his feet and the gentle rustling of the trees calmed him. But most of all, he loved to climb a tall dune and look up at the sky, where billions of stars sparkled.

One night, as he gazed at the stars as usual, a particularly bright star fell from the sky, leaving a trail of golden stardust. Curiously, Enzo followed the path of stardust.

He wandered through the forest, across meadows and rivers, until he eventually reached a small pond. There, in the midst of the pond, he saw the fallen star shimmering in the water. Carefully, Enzo stretched out his trunk, touched the star, and lifted it up.

To his surprise, the star began to speak: "Thank you, Enzo. I lost my way in the sky and fell down. But now, that you've found me, I can return to the sky."

Enzo was astonished but happy to be able to help the star. He quietly wished for the star to return safely to its place. In a bright, golden light, the star soared back up into the sky and took its place among the other stars.

Enzo returned to his home, with the feeling that he had experienced something truly magical that night. And every time he looked up at the sky at night, that one star sparkled a little brighter, as a sign of gratitude to the little elephant.

Dear children, no matter how small we feel, we can always do great things and help others. Sleep well now and dream of magical starry nights. Good night!

The Dreaming Fox

In a cozy fox den, deep in the heart of a dense forest, lived a little fox named Felix. Felix wasn't like the other foxes. While most dreamed of being the fastest runners or hunters, Felix had a different dream: he wanted to tell the most beautiful stories.

Every evening, as the sun set, Felix sat on a small hill and gazed at the stars. He dreamed of the incredible stories he could tell. Stories of adventures, brave heroes, and distant lands. The other foxes laughed at Felix and his dream. "Foxes are hunters, not storytellers," they said. "Give up this silly dream."

Felix didn't let himself be discouraged. He believed in his dream and in himself. So, he began working on his stories. The fox listened to the tales of the birds, observed the activities in the forest, and let his imagination run wild. Every evening, more and more animals gathered around him to listen to his stories.

One day, after Felix had told an especially exciting story, loud applause broke out. Even the skeptical foxes who had once laughed at him came to him and asked him to tell more stories. Felix understood that it wasn't about being like the other foxes but about pursuing his own dreams.

The story of Felix, the storyteller, teaches us that it's important to believe in our dreams and pursue them, no matter what others say. It's not about meeting others' expectations but about doing what fulfills us and brings us happiness.

Anton and the Moon Song

In a deep, dense jungle where tall trees reached almost to the sky and colorful birds fluttered among the leaves, lived Anton, a small cheerful monkey. Anton had big, curious eyes and soft, fluffy fur.

What set Anton apart was his love for music. Every evening, when the moon was in the sky, Anton would climb the tallest tree he could find and drum with his small hands on a hollow tree trunk drum.

The other animals in the jungle knew it was time for Anton's moon song when they heard the drum. They would all gather around the tree and listen to the rhythmic sounds and gentle singing of Anton.

One evening, as the monkey played his song, he noticed that the moon seemed especially bright and close. It almost felt like the moon was coming down to listen to him.

With each beat of his drum, the moon came closer and closer, until it hovered directly above Anton, bathing the whole land in a soft, silvery light.

For a moment, the entire jungle listened as Anton and the moon sang their song together. It was the most beautiful duet the animals had ever heard.

When the song came to an end, the moon slowly climbed back into the sky, and the animals clapped and cheered with joy. They thanked the monkey for the beautiful song and then went to sleep, feeling a sense of peace and happiness in their hearts.

Anton snuggled into his favorite tree and fell into a deep and restful sleep, dreaming of moonlight and music.

Dear children, remember that music can work wonders. Dream sweet dreams and good night!

The Little Mouse

34

Once upon a time, there was a small, clever mouse named Mimi who lived in a peaceful field. One day, while she was searching for food, she stumbled upon something unusual. It was a huge elephant named Edgar, peacefully sleeping under a tree.

Carefully, Mimi approached the sleeping elephant. She had never seen such a large animal before! When Edgar woke up and saw the mouse, he smiled and greeted her warmly. Mimi was surprised - she hadn't expected such a large creature to be so gentle and polite.

Despite their size difference, Mimi and Edgar found similarities. They both loved the fresh morning air, the crunch of leaves under their feet, and the rustling of the wind in the trees. The two played together in the field, shared their meals, and listened to each other when one was feeling sad.

The other mice couldn't understand why Mimi was friends with an elephant. "He's so big, and you're so small," they said. "How can you be friends?" But Mimi just smiled and replied, "Our hearts are equally big."

The days passed, and the friendship between Mimi and Edgar grew stronger and stronger. They stood up for each other and learned from one another. The mouse taught the elephant to be gentle and patient, while Edgar taught Mimi to be brave and confident.

The story of the two teaches us that friendship knows no boundaries. It doesn't matter how big or small, young or old we are. What matters is accepting differences, sharing similarities, and being there for each other. True friendship doesn't see size; it sees the heart.

Vivi and the Moon

In a small nest, atop the tallest tree in a vast forest, lived Vivi, a young bird. Vivi had soft, colorful feathers and knew a melodic song that she often trilled. But what Vivi loved the most was the moon. Every night, she would look up and admire its gentle glow.

One evening, Vivi noticed that the moon wasn't shining as brightly as usual. She grew concerned, wondering if something had happened to the moon. The little bird decided to get as close to the moon as possible and check on it.

She fluttered higher and higher through the cool night air, until she felt she could almost touch the moon. To her surprise, Vivi discovered a small cloud positioned right in front of the moon, casting a shadow over it.

With her tiny wings, she gently pushed the cloud aside. The moon started shining again, brighter and more beautiful than ever.

"Thank you, dear little bird," said the moon. "I had been hiding behind that cloud because I was feeling shy. But now, with your help, I can shine again with full brilliance for everyone."

Vivi was happy that she could help. She sang a cheerful song and danced in the moonlight.

After bidding farewell, Vivi returned to her nest and fell asleep peacefully, comforted by the knowledge that the moon was watching over her.

Good night, little dreamers. Close your eyes, let the moon lull you to sleep, and dream of celestial adventures.

The Brave Squirrel

A little squirrel named Timmy lived in a dense, green forest. He was known for his cheerful nature and his ability to keep a smile on his face in every situation. But one day, the squirrel faced a great challenge.

The sky turned dark, and clouds rolled in. A big storm was approaching. All the other animals in the forest quickly sought shelter, but Timmy hadn't gathered food for the winter yet.

He knew he had to venture out and gather food despite the storm. With his little heart full of courage, he set out on his journey. The wind was strong, and the rain pelted his fur, but Timmy wasn't deterred.

The squirrel leaped from tree to tree, collecting nuts and berries despite the danger the storm posed. After hours of hard work and with a supply of food, he began his journey back.

Exhausted but content, Timmy returned to his tree stump. He had succeeded. He had gathered enough food for the winter and faced the challenge of the storm.

This story teaches children the value of courage and the importance of preparing for challenging times. Timmy showed that in times of difficulty, it's important to be brave and to prepare for what lies ahead. Through his bravery, Timmy was able to sustain himself and his family through the winter.

Imprint

Texts: © Nadine Lichtenegger
Address: Waldstraße 20d, 8793 Trofaiach, Austria
Email: nadlichti06@gmx.at

Cover Design: Marie from mw@wolkenart.com
Book Layout: Red Heads

All rights reserved.
Reproduction, even in part, is not permitted.

The work, including its parts, is protected by copyright. Any use without the consent of the publisher and the author is prohibited. This applies especially to electronic or other reproduction, translation, distribution, and public accessibility.